Our Lady

A PRESENTATION
FOR BEGINNERS

OUR Lady

A Presentation for Beginners

DOM HUBERT VAN ZELLER, O.S.B.

AROUCA PRESS

Nihil Obstat:
Ralph Russell, o.s.b., Censor Deputatus
Imprimatur:
B. C. Butler, Abb. Praes.
8 September 1962

First Published 1963 by Templegate Publishers
Copyright © Downside Abbey General Trust
(Permission granted for this republication)

ISBN 978-1-99947-295-5 (pbk)

Arouca Press
PO Box 55003
Bridgeport PO
Waterloo, ON N2J3G0
Canada
www.aroucapress.com
Send inquiries to info@aroucapress.com

Book and cover design
by Michael Schrauzer

For Barbette and Fleur

CONTENTS

FOREWORD

WHEN THEOLOGY IS PLACED IN THE hands of a master, something like *Our Lady, A Presentation for Beginners* results.

What makes someone a master of theology? Many things come to mind, such as orthodoxy. But a quality of orthodox theology is not the mere parroting of what has already been taught; it demands thought — original ideas — coming at the subject with fresh eyes. It has other qualities too, and when you read Dom Hubert van Zeller, you have all these qualities in abundance.

For example, clarity is one quality that is essential for good theology. Dom Hubert has the knack of getting right to the point with clarity, without being wordy. Take the opening lines for example:

> When the angel Gabriel spoke to our Lady at the Annunciation the name "Mary" was not used; it was the Church that added the name when the Hail Mary was composed. There was no need for Gabriel to call our Lady by her name because the words "full of grace" amounted to a name. Since nobody else had been full of grace in the whole of

history it was a proper name in the strictest sense. It was as if the angel, knowing about the Immaculate Conception, was giving her the name which best suited the part she was playing in the plan of God.

There you have it. This is clear as a bell, and accessible to anyone who can read. You don't find any jargon; no reliance on obscure German phrases (or Greek or Latin for that matter); no reliance on esoteric philosophy, yet simultaneously he achieves much depth in just a few words. You could meditate on just that passage for several days and profit from it.

If he does mention a particularly theological word like "incarnation," he will stop to explain it, but not with some definition taken from a book. For example, when he introduces the subject of the Incarnation he says, "At first sight, when we read that God made Mary holy for His own sake and to suit the plan He had in mind, there is the slight feeling of shock. We cannot avoid the thought that if one of us did something like that there would be a certain sense of guilt about it, a certain touch of selfishness. But obviously there cannot be guilt or selfishness where God is concerned. In preparing Mary for the Incarnation it was not like preparing the best sort of throne for himself—just for the satisfaction of being able to rule from it. (If that had been the case He would hardly have chosen a stable as His throne-room or a cross from which to reign.) No,

Mary was made perfect because only through a door which had never for an instant been closed to grace could He who was all good come into the world."

And what respect he has for the subject! This is present in any of his works, and may be found in abundance in this work. Respect I would say, and yes, much love. Here is an author that loves the subject, and is as far from the technician in a lab coat with his dissecting tools peering at the frog as St. Joseph was when he first looked at his Betrothed.

Clarity, light, respect, fidelity, love; these are the qualities which Dom Hubert brings to his subject, with a plain but profound and direct illumination of "Our tainted nature's solitary boast," as Wordsworth called Our Lady. What a little treasure is this book!

— The Rev. James W. Jackson, FSSP
Pastor, Our Lady of Mt. Carmel Parish
Littleton, Colorado

CHAPTER I

Hail Mary,
Full of Grace

WHEN THE ANGEL Gabriel spoke to our Lady at the Annunciation the name 'Mary' was not used; it was the Church that added the name when the *Hail Mary* was composed. There was no need for Gabriel to call our Lady by her name because the words 'full of grace' amounted to a name. Since nobody else had been full of grace in the whole of history it was a proper name in the strictest sense. It was as if the angel, knowing about the Immaculate Conception, was giving her the name which best suited the part she was playing in the plan of God. You can think of it as Gabriel saying to Mary: 'I salute you, O Full-of-Grace, as the one most perfectly prepared for the message which you shall hear.' There was no part of Mary's soul that was not entirely occupied by grace. Original sin had never been there to make crevices in her soul where selfishness might lurk.

Holy as Mary was both before the Annunciation and after, her holiness was not of her own making. The same is true of all holy people: they have not come to holiness by the strength of their wills. Whatever is good about you or me is put there by God, is His present to us. We know from Scripture that we cannot even call upon the holy name of Jesus in prayer unless we are given the grace to do it. So Mary's holiness was God's gift to her — as she tells us distinctly in the *Magnificat*. At every moment Mary was ready for God's grace, ready to be holy in whatever way God would choose, but she would never have been holy if God's grace had not come along and made her so.

If it had not been adopted by others, the symbol of the moon and the star would be a good one for us to give our Lady. The moon's light is a borrowed light, and so also is the light of the star which is sheltered within the protecting curve of the moon. All light — Mary's goodness as well as the goodness of lesser beings like ourselves whom she shelters against the darkness of the night — comes from the sun. Unfortunately the idea cannot be carried any further because of course the crescent is only that bit of the moon which happens to be facing the sun and so gets lit up. In Mary's case, the whole of her is facing the sun, and all her soul is lit by grace.

If this were better understood, and if we made it clear that the beauty of Mary was the reflected beauty of God, perhaps those outside the Church would come to honor her more. Non-Catholics would then see that we do not worship Mary as a kind of separate sun, as though she possessed a light which she herself had made and which shone independently of anything else, but that we see her always as the most favored of beings under Him from whom all goodness comes.

Why did God make Mary so holy, so much more holy than anyone else? Why did He allow no stain of original sin on her soul when all the rest of us come into the world with it? The answer is that He did it for His own sake: He made her spotless because she was to be the mother of His own Son. If the Second Person of the Blessed Trinity was to be born of a human being, then that human being must be made perfect. Sin, whether original or actual must have no place in her.

At first sight, when we read that God made Mary holy for His own sake and to suit the plan He had in mind, there is the slight feeling of shock. We cannot avoid the thought that if one of us did something like that there would be a certain sense of guilt about it, a certain touch of selfishness. But obviously there cannot be guilt or selfishness where God is concerned. In preparing Mary for the Incarnation it was not like preparing the best sort of throne for himself — just for the satisfaction of being able to rule from it. (If that had been the case He would hardly have chosen a stable as His throne-room or a cross from which to reign.) No, Mary was made perfect because only through a door which had never for an instant been closed to grace could He who was all good come into the world.

Perfect humility and perfect love *had* to be the setting for the Incarnation. The word 'incarnation' means 'enfleshment' — the taking of a human body. For the infinite goodness of God to take human shape, reaching the world by means of a human mother's body, the ordinary state of fallen beings like the rest of us could never have been good enough to borrow from: our Lord's sinless body and soul had to come by means of a body and soul which also had never known sin. So, all along, Mary was full of grace. Full of grace because her Son was full of grace.

But it was not *only* for the sake of a perfect Incarnation that God made Mary perfect. That was the most necessary reason for her holiness, but since holiness never stops short at serving a single object there were others besides God for whose sake Mary was perfected. It was for her own sake too, and for ours. Holiness cannot be something hoarded and privately enjoyed. It is not like a sum of money, locked in a cashbox and taken out only to spend on buying personal gifts for God. Holiness is something which is shared, and the more it is given out to others the more it is multiplied in the soul.

Holiness, grace, charity: these things are not lessened in your store but increased when you distribute them. It is not like giving away a book and leaving a gap on your shelf. It is more like giving away some of your blood to a patient who is having a blood-transfusion: the sacrifice draws up more into your veins. Now although Mary was full of grace before the Annunciation, she became able to carry greater grace after it. More and more grace was poured into her soul by God as she grew older. As her needs grew — the care of our Lord demanded more each day — her spiritual intake grew too. And with her spiritual intake growing every day, she responded more and more so that her holiness was mounting all the time.

God always gives us the grace to fulfill our vocation. If it is a vocation to something great (like martyrdom or the religious life or bringing up a large and holy family), great graces will be given to fulfill it. Obviously, if you decide to be a gambler or a gangster you are not going to get the graces which God gives to someone who chooses to be a saintly priest or a saintly parent. You may want to be a perfect gunman, but since God has higher ideas about what you can be He gives you exactly the right graces for the career you decide to follow. So if you happen to become a gunman, which God does not want but which He still gives you the free will to choose if you are such a fool as to go against His wishes, you can at least count on the grace to be converted back from being a gunman — and on the grace to stay out of mortal sin in the meantime. Perhaps you will not act on the graces that are given you, and if you stay on as a gunman you probably will not want to, but anyway you must always know that God has not forgotten you. He is loving you the whole time and is only waiting for you to return His love.

In Mary's case the response to God's love was complete, uninterrupted, always growing. Throughout her life she was giving in to God's will and asking for more. Her surrender was joyous, loving, unquestioning. And in her union with God she was never so carried away with her own happiness as not to remember the needs of other people. If it was like that during her lifetime on earth, it has been like that ever since. She who was the mother of mankind (because she was the mother of Him in whom mankind belongs) carries always in her prayer the needs of her countless millions of children.

It should be enormously comforting to us when we think how Mary is all the time offering to the Father her merits and intercessions in which we, individually, have a place. It is not even as though the whole human race were just lumped together and prayed for under a general intention. Mary is the mother of each one of us, pleading for the salvation and sanctification of every soul. And because God has made her full of grace, He cannot turn away from her prayer. He is the love which makes her prayer, so He could not possibly turn away from it.

CHAPTER 2

The Lord Is With Thee

WHEN GABRIEL hailed Mary with the words 'the Lord is with thee' it was more than just a greeting. People to this day in Palestine, and in other countries where religion is part of daily life, salute one another in such ways. Where we say 'How d'you do' (or, more shortly, 'Hi'), men and women who have a better sense of God's presence say things like 'Blessed be God' and 'May you bring the Lord' and 'God be with you.' There was nothing strange about Mary being addressed in this way. What was strange was that this time it was absolutely and strictly and theologically true.

Not only at the moment of the Annunciation was

God with Mary in a closer and more wonderful way than He had been with anyone else in the whole long history of man, but He had been with her all along. Her soul had never, since the first moment of its existence, *not* been with Him. In the case of our souls, we have to be bought back by the merits of Christ, which baptism lets us share, from the state of slavery into which original sin has sold us. Baptism brings us into the body of Christ from outside. But with Mary there was no question of ever being 'outside': she was united to God from the beginning.

'The Lord is with thee' became even more true from the instant of Mary's acceptance of the angel's message. In a very special way was God with her and she with God. As she had lived in union with the Father throughout her girlhood, now Jesus was beginning to live His life in her. Even before He was born, the Second Person in the Blessed Trinity was alive in Mary's sinless body. So if at the beginning of the Annunciation the angel Gabriel was speaking generally of God when he said 'the Lord is with thee,' he could have meant Jesus in a very special way by the end of it.

✠

And in a very special way Jesus remained with her ever since. Our Lord was with Mary until He was born on Christmas Day, was with her when the Holy Family fled into Egypt, was with her again at Nazareth, in Jerusalem, at Cana, was with her during His ministry, during His Passion and Crucifixion. Before He died He entrusted her to the care of St. John, but in death He did not leave her. When the darkness lifted, she was still there under the cross waiting to receive His body. Gabriel's words 'the Lord is with thee' could have been said to her at any moment since the Annunciation.

Nor was Mary separated from her Son during the years that followed His death. Sacramentally she received Him from the hands of St John, but even if Holy Communion had been denied to her she would have been united with Him in her soul. 'The Lord is with thee' still held — whether at Mass or while moving about her tiny house (vouched for by one tradition) at Ephesus. Then the Assumption, the Coronation before the Father's throne, and after it, the everlasting place she occupies today as Queen. 'The Lord is with thee': it applies now as much as ever, and so will go on applying for all eternity.

This book does not set out to teach you either history or catechism or scripture. But in explaining about the part played by Our Lady in the Christian idea of religion, it has no intention of sticking so closely to the subject as to pass by all that does not point directly to the Blessed Mother. To know how Mary has been shown by various artists, for instance, or at different times in history and by different races: these things can help to give us a wider understanding of Mary's position in the Church, and to understand more should lead to loving more. So long as we are trying to improve our service and devotion to Mary, the more information we have about her the better.

To start off with, it is worth noticing how the Church has picked out many places in the Old Testament — whole chapters which were written hundreds of years before Mary was born — which are applied to the Mother of God. If you read the eighth chapter of the Book of Proverbs you will see how Mary is like to the 'wisdom' which was in the mind of God during the creation of the World. 'I was with Him forming all things,' you will read in the thirtieth verse. Does not this fit in perfectly with Gabriel's 'The Lord is with thee'?

In the Old Testament, still under the figure of wisdom, Mary's place is in the clouds: she dwells in contemplation, pondering the works of God's hands. Does not this fit in perfectly with the account of her which we get in the New Testament: 'treasuring all these things in her heart'? In the one it is the Father's acts that occupy her prayer; in the other it is the Son's. The Lord is with her in prophecy just as He is with her in Palestine.

Then there is the name which the Church gives to Mary, calling her the second Eve. This title is full of ideas to be followed up. With Mary playing the part of another Eve, the whole story of the Fall is put in reverse. Just as Eve prepared the way for man's sin, so Mary prepares the way for man's redemption; just as

Eve was seen to have listened to the voice of the serpent, so Mary is seen as crushing the serpent's head; just as Eve lingered by the forbidden tree in Eden's garden, so Mary stands by the cross of perfect obedience on Calvary; just as Eve was driven from Paradise by an angel, so angels accompany Mary on her Way to eternal Paradise at her Assumption. The very name Eve, so the Bible tells us, means 'mother of all living,' and this is just what Mary, the second Eve, became.

Through Mary we get back much, but not all, that we had lost through Eve. The Fall meant banishment for man, and we are still banished from the perfect natural happiness which might have been ours. But with Mary to prepare the entry of our Lord into the world we have a mother who prepares us for our entry into heaven. When we pray in the *Salve Regina* 'to thee do we cry, poor banished children of Eve,' we are not really so poor as we think. If Mary's Son had not redeemed us we would be *really* banished — banished from eternal life with Him in heaven — and now we are not. We are just exiles for a time, and even now we can count on the companionship of Jesus and Mary. As the second 'mother of the living,' Mary helps us more than the first mother, Eve, ever would have done. Mary came closer to God than Eve did, and loved more. Mary passed the great test of love, humility, obedience; Eve did not.

So you see we have no reason to pine away with longing for an earthly paradise which is closed to us because of the Fall; nothing can open up that place again so we might as well stop worrying about it. The thing to do is to see what we have got instead. We have got the promise of eternal happiness, we have got the merits of Christ which will bring us to eternal happiness if we do our part in His service, we have got His Holy Spirit in the Church to guide us and tell us about truth, we have got the Blessed Sacrament in our tabernacles (and we can remember that even before the Fall there was no Holy Communion, while after the Fall not even the holiest of souls whose lives are described in the Old Testament had the graces which come to us in the sacraments), *and* we have got Mary.

If Eve and her husband walked with God in the garden, the second Eve and her Son walk with the Father in heaven. 'The Lord is with thee' has come to mean more than it meant when Gabriel first spoke the words. Moreover she walks with us, drawing us always closer to her Son and sheltering us from the harm which in this life is never far off. If only we could learn to respond to her love, as a child responds to its mother's, we would never have anything to fear from the dangers which surround us. From her we would learn more about our Lord, because He is with her, and we would learn too to take our ideas about life not from the world but from the places with which she was most connected: Bethlehem, Nazareth, Calvary. 'Hail, full of grace,' we would say, 'the Lord is with thee, and we would ask Him to be with us too.

I do not know much about queens but I do know
something about mothers: I want to be a proper son
to you. I do not know much about the next life, but
I do know something about this present one;
I want to make proper use of my time
on earth. You can help me. Please
do. Amen.' That is the
kind of thing we
would say.

CHAPTER 3

Blessed Art Thou Among Women

HE FIRST THING
that strikes us about this third
sentence in Gabriel's opening
speech to Mary is the way she is
described as being still — in spite of her
wonderful graces — among women. Her holiness may
be above the holiness of all other women, her immaculate conception may be something which no other
woman can expect to enjoy, but she is one of her kind
all the same. If Gabriel had said 'blessed art thou
beyond women,' which would have been perfectly true,
we might have had the sneaking feeling that it would
be no good trying to follow her. But having her
described like this as *among* women brings her far
closer, and makes her example far more practical.

We have seen already how Mary is the mother of all mankind, men and women and children. But because she is a woman she is of course especially the model for womanhood and motherhood. Standing particularly for the race of woman, Mary shows to all the world what her sex is meant to be like. If she is to crush the serpent's head, it must be women who do it with her. If she is to rest her feet upon the moon, having the twelve stars about her, it must be for women to share the light of her purity and to shine with the particular virtues of their state.

The sad thing is that women are inclined to forget that they are expected to show a likeness to Mary. They often show a respect, a confidence, a compassion, a gratitude. But do they as often try to show any actual *resemblance*? It is true they are made first in the image and likeness of God; but they are also made in the image and likeness of Mary. At least they can grow into that image and likeness. 'Blessed art thou among women': they too can be blessed in their degree.

So it is not much good having a devotion to Mary if her example means nothing to you. Unless you aim at thinking as she thinks, at doing what you feel pretty sure she would do, at avoiding the evils which you know must displease her, you are not really serving her at all. True devotion to Mary is not stuffing your prayer-books with pictures of her, putting madonna statues in every room, clinking a rosary as you come into church, building grottoes and shrines in the garden. True devotion to Mary is trying to love God as she does, trying to do for the world what she is doing. Outward devotions can help, and they may well be true signs of the real thing inside, but imitation of Mary is far more pleasing to God and to her than a truckload of pious objects.

A famous and learned archbishop has recently said in a pastoral letter to his diocese in France: 'The most powerful moral force in the world is the modern girl.' This is not just a headline, written to startle. It is a serious conclusion arrived at by a serious man of God. Now a moral force can work either way, for good or for evil. And if the girl is as powerful in the world as the archbishop thinks she is, she must know how to go about her girlhood. She must take her lead from our Lady in other words, and not from the stars and queens of worldliness. She must know that Mary represents her race, is the ideal proposed to every member of her sex, stands beside her in girlhood, womanhood, motherhood. Is the modern girl going to take up the challenge, modelling herself on Mary's purity, or is she going to repeat all the old excuses which worldly people give to explain their worldliness — and so let go of Mary's summons and example altogether? We must pray to our Lady that she may guide 'the most powerful force in the world' towards her Son and away from the morals which the prince of darkness is trying to get accepted by mankind.

✠

If it may sound a little bit distant and unreal to speak of Mary up in heaven, queen of all the saints, gently shepherding the human race towards its rightful place in the plan of God (which is what in fact she was doing) we can bring the idea closer by seeing her as doing it for each of us separate human beings. You and I personally, because we are members of humanity at large, are the special objects of Mary's care. If our Lord and St Paul speak of us as branches of Christ's vine and members of His body, then even the smallest living particles of that vine and that body can expect to be looked after by the mother of Jesus.

Forget for the moment how humanity broke away from God at the Fall. Forget how humanity has got to get itself fitted back again into its state of creaturely obedience if it is to inherit the Creator's promise. These are important subjects which have to be gone into some time, but at this stage they are inclined to confuse. Say to yourself quite simply: '*I* was parted from God by my first parents . . . *I* am a part of our Lord's body . . . Mary brought our Lord's body into the world . . . our Lord, by including *me* in the merits of His Passion, has restored *me* to the Father . . . so I can truly say that through Mary's motherhood comes the means of my salvation, and that right through my life I am being watched over and helped by Mary, who watched over and helped Him of whom I am a member.'

To watch and help in this way is Mary's chief work for souls on earth. Though our Lord is glorified in heaven, not all the living cells of His body are glorified in heaven. Belonging as we do to the Church Militant, we have yet to win our way to glory. But while striving here on earth we have the whole force of Mary's holiness on our side. How could it be otherwise? Must she not fight on the side of her Son? Must she not protect the members of her Son's body which are still exposed to danger? And when those members, wounded and weak, have joined the Church Suffering before they finally appear before the throne of God in glory, must she not constantly be praying for them in Purgatory?

So it comes to this, then, that Mary's holiness shows itself everywhere: on earth for us; in Purgatory for the holy souls; in heaven for the greater glory of God. Blessed is she not only among women but among all souls — whether struggling, suffering, or triumphant. Not until we are united with God in heaven shall we be able to see what our Lady has been doing for us all along. It will surely be one of the joys of heaven to find ourselves tracing with gratitude the course of her care of us over the past.

Perhaps only a mother can really know what a woman must have to go through with on account of her son. All we can do here is to guess that if she was 'blessed among women,' Mary must have suffered among women the same pains and sorrows and anxieties. But in her case these griefs were a million times more deep because her soul was a million times deeper than any other mother's.

Think of what it must have meant to Mary to know that her Son's teaching was rejected by the very people, the priests and the religious authorities, who should have listened to it and encouraged others to listen. Think of her feelings when she heard, as she must have done, the crowds cry out for His death, and when they chose for release 'not this man but Barabbas.' Put yourself in her place when she met Him carrying the cross on the way to Calvary, when she saw Him being prepared for crucifixion, when she heard Him being hammered to the wood, when she watched Him during His last hour of life, when she saw that He was dead. 'Blessed art thou among women'; no woman has had so much to suffer as you.

If she has sorrowed over the agonies of her divine Son, she has suffered too over the agonies of her human sons — us sinners. As Mother of Compassion it is not only Christ whom she compassionates. Her love goes out to us with the same love of the mother for her children. Just as Christ bore our sins upon himself and entered into our sufferings, so Mary who has been called the co-redemptrix (though this teaching has not been defined as an article of faith) takes upon herself her share in her Son's whole atoning

work. You have seen her in pictures with seven swords
pointing to her heart? She draws them to herself in
compassion and reparation. She invites the wounds
which we are not strong enough to bear. It is just
what a mother would do. 'Blessed art thou
among women' — more blessed
than any who have borne the
sins and sorrows of
their children.

CHAPTER 4

Blessed is the Fruit of Thy Womb

ERHAPS YOU have sometimes wondered about the text which says that 'the Word was made flesh and dwelt among us.' (The text is from the first chapter of St John's Gospel, and is familiar because it comes at Christmas and at the end of Mass.) Why does the text say that the 'Word' became flesh? Why not, 'the Second Person of the Blessed Trinity' was made flesh—or simply 'God'? Well, the answer is that the 'word' here is not just a spoken or written Word, but is taken to stand for the idea *behind* what may be spoken or written. So although the Incarnation is truly the Word of God made flesh, it is more easily understood when we think of the divine idea coming from our God's mind and expressing itself in the human body of our Lord. The *idea* is there all along, the *expressing* takes place, and the Word dwells among us in the flesh.

And if you have followed that first stiff paragraph you will see what is meant when Mary is called Mother of the Word. The true idea of God, existing eternally in the divine mind, is translated from heaven to earth through the womb of the Blessed Virgin Mary. Just like a word translated from one language to another, the word of God is translated from one kind of living to another. Before He was made flesh the Son of God did not dwell among us; after the first Christmas He did. So of course Gabriel could say 'blessed is the fruit of thy womb.' The fruit was the living Word.

A certain writer who was famous in ancient China for his wisdom spoke about God as 'the womb of his own thought.' To an oriental mind it is always the thought, the idea, that is the important thing. Out of the hidden thought comes the object or the act or the speech which we can see and hear. Perhaps that wise man of China would have understood the doctrine of the Immaculate Conception if it had been put to him. Certainly he would have agreed with the Christian claim that the eternal Word of God could take shape in the human womb of Mary, and that from this wholly pure womb He would issue as God and man.

The people of far eastern lands have a different way of looking at things than we have, and perhaps it is a better way. If we had the same point of view about material goods we might not be so greedy for them. Certainly we would not judge them to be as important as the idea which brought them about. Where the thought is valued above all, there is far less difficulty in taking on all that concerns faith and hope and love. Outward things, material objects, are to the oriental mind no more than the shell, the visible covering of what really matters. When they think of a jar or bottle they think of the space inside which takes the shape of the jar; when they think of a temple they think of the room there is to pray and walk about in, and not of the walls and roof as we would; when they think of a wheel they think not of the rim but of what the rim encloses. It is a more sensible way of thinking but, though we need not try to imitate this view, we ought to feel encouraged to pray that eastern lands will one day accept Christianity. To minds which look below the surface appearance, and search out the real meaning of what is seen and heard and handled, the doctrine of the Blessed Sacrament would bring no difficulties. And 'blessed is the fruit of thy womb,' the divine Word or Idea coming forth blessed from the human covering of Mary's immaculate womb to dwell among us as a human being like ourselves — would seem to them the most natural thing in the world.

So we should pray for the conversion of those eastern religions to the true faith, asking our Lady to bring from her womb the graces which will prepare souls for the Incarnation. Along with the well-founded belief among Catholics that Mary is co-redemptrix is the belief that she is also mediatrix of all graces. This second claim makes Mary the channel of every grace that comes from Christ to man, so if this is the case we can rely upon her not only to take up our petition but also to be the means of seeing the petition fulfilled. Mary, mother of God, bring your Son to the East. May He be better served in the East than by what He has received from us in the West. May the faith and devotion with which these earnest non-Christians pray to their gods be brought to focus upon our Lord. May God be glorified in all His nations.

✠

In the Greek Church our Lady is particularly honored as Living Temple of God. This title is worth looking into because it makes Mary not merely the human means by which our Lord came into the world, but the dwelling place of God's Holy Spirit in the world today. As mother of the Church she is thought of as carrying on the work of the Incarnation. Just as our Lord is in His Church, so is Mary; and 'she who is greater than the heavens' lives among the faithful as their mother.

In Greek art this special activity of Mary (which gives to her the name 'Empsychos') is shown in a way which has been fixed by tradition. She is seen full-face, and with both hands raised; she wears a blue tunic and a red cloak; there are three stars about her, and our Lord is seen in a circle of light against her breast. The fact that she is not represented side-face or in profile is meant to show that she keeps all under her constant gaze: She looks out over the whole world. The blue of her tunic stands for her humanity, and the red of her cloak for the abiding protection of the Holy Spirit. The raised hands means prayer — praise and intercession especially — and the three stars express the threefold quality of her chastity. Mary is *ever* virgin: before the Nativity, during it, after it.

So you see the Greeks are inclined to plan things out much more than we are. We in Western Christianity tend to paint or carve Mary as the fancy moves us. The Greeks work out our Lady's position in theology and express it as closely as they can in symbols. We think of Mary as the Madonna, the young mother in the stable at Bethlehem, the mother on Calvary weeping over her dead Son. To the Greeks she is first the Mother of God (which gives her the name 'Theotokos'), and only then, because she is mother of the whole Christ, head and members, is she thought of as ministering to the everyday needs of her human sons and daughters. It is just a different way of looking at things, and though it comes to the same in the end we ought to be glad that our way of looking at things makes Mary a much easier person to go to with our troubles.

We have this great advantage, that when we pray 'Blessed art thou among women and blessed is the fruit of thy womb,' we can feel at home with her. We are not being instructed, we are being understood. Other Christian churches than ours might be puzzled by Lourdes and Fatima. These places do not puzzle us a bit. They add to our love of Mary because we see at close quarters how Mary's love for her children is expressed. We see the link between her love for Jesus and her love for us. We see that these are not two loves but one. Perhaps because other Christian churches do not quite see this, and think instead that we worship Mary as a sort of human goddess, there are souls who love our Lord but who are doing without graces which we can have for the asking. All the more reason why we should beg Him and His holy mother to open out to them the way of grace which always lies open to us. Through the womb of Mary comes to us our life — and with this life in Christ come hope and peace and trust.

✠

Just as the name 'Mary' was not mentioned by Gabriel, so neither was the name 'Jesus.' In adding both these names to the *Hail Mary* the devotion of the faithful has followed the ordinary course of affection. When we are fond of people we like to repeat their names. The very sound of their names seems to brings them closer. Conversation and correspondence would

become cold indeed if the people addressed were never
called upon by name. Prayers in the same way would
become cold and dull. And one of the first things
we have to learn in the service of God is that
prayer is a conversation, *is* a correspondence — and that it is one affection-
ate intimacy. So 'Hail Mary
. . . blessed is the fruit
of thy womb,
Jesus.'

CHAPTER 5

*Holy Mary,
Mother of God*

ROM NOW
until the end of the
prayer there is a different feel about the *Hail Mary*.
Gabriel has stopped speaking, and the devotion of the
faithful has begun to express itself. The prayer has
taken a new direction, changing from statements of
fact to direct appeal. It is true that this opening phrase
of the second part states a fact too, but if you look
carefully at the words which follow you will see that
Mary is being addressed as 'mother of God' for a particular reason — so that she may use her influence with
God in gaining for us the graces which must reward
her prayer. We give to Mary her strictly theological
title, and then ask her to act according to her status
by interceding for us.

When we call Mary 'holy,' each of us probably has a different idea about what such holiness means. To one person the Mother of God may appeal as possessing the holiness of all the saints put together; to another the word 'holy' may give the idea of being saintly in a very special and particular way. What most of us would agree upon is that Mary's own gift of holiness to mankind was the way she fell in with God's plan. *From* this flow all the virtues which we know were hers. She was humble, she was obedient, she trusted, she loved, she prayed, she suffered for the love of God; but the key to all her holiness lies in what she said when Gabriel had delivered his message. 'Behold the handmaid of the Lord,' she said, 'be it done unto me according to thy will.'

Now when you think about it, you see that all holiness is just simply that: being ready to accept whatever God wants. Nor is this a matter of taking on God's will because it must happen anyway and it is no good trying to get out of it. It is a matter of going to meet it lovingly. Mary was ready for anything, and when the anything became something special she lovingly devoted herself to it.

So often we think of people as being 'holy' because they *do* 'holy' things or *say* 'holy' things, but really we should think of holiness as giving in to God over everything — even when He decides that doing and saying holy things is ruled out for us. Before Gabriel appeared, Mary must have planned her life of service to God. She may have had all sorts of grand notions as to how she would express her love — in ministering to the poor and sick of Jerusalem, for instance, or in living the life of solitude and prayer — the moment she learned of God's will for her there was only one course open. She dropped her own ideas and set about being perfect according to God's idea. And that is the whole secret of holiness.

If you can shape your life according to Mary's 'be it done to me as God wills' you have found the answer not only to the problem of holiness but also to the problem of human well-being. People who take life as coming from the hand of God are never upset by troubles and are always ready for the next thing. They are grateful for the joys, because the joys are a sign of God's love, and they are equally ready to make the best of the sorrows, because the sorrows are seen as being a part-share in the sacred Passion. So the more you try to model yourself on the answer which Mary gave to Gabriel the nearer you will get to the holiness which God wants to see in His subjects. Mary was *holy* Mary for a hundred reasons, but chiefly she was holy because there was no part of God's will that she did not accept with all her heart. The whole of Mary's soul went out in welcome to the whole of God's design.

Now there is just this to be noticed before we go on to the next bit. Mary may not have known the details of God's design, may not have had any idea how far her act of generosity would lead her, but this did not matter. What mattered was that she threw her soul open to the complete and un-restricted way of grace. Her acceptance did not depend on her knowledge of the future; her acceptance came straight from her love. The example of Mary should encourage us when we feel that there is something which God wants, and when at the same time we are not at all sure about how it will turn out. Those are just the times when we should accept, trust, and go straight on. The call to do something for God is bound to carry with it the grace to fulfil the call. Mary was 'holy' because she believed this and acted upon it. One reason why the rest of us are not holy is that we are never quite sure whether we believe it or not, and in any case do not act on it.

A thing that stands out prominently about Mary's holiness — and yet is so much a part of it that you cannot think of one without the other — is her humility. Mary even speaks of her own 'lowliness,' and to do this you have to be either very humble indeed or else a hypocrite. The truth is that Mary saw herself so clearly as the instrument of God's will, as a soul loaded with graces which were purely God's gift, that she could stand back from herself and talk about her humility as if it were a virtue which belonged to somebody else. In a sense it *was* a virtue which belonged to somebody else — it belonged to God and was lent to her. The same is the case with whatever virtues we happen to possess: none of them is of our own making; we cannot invent our own virtues, we can only develop them under grace.

If you read the *Magnificat* slowly through, thinking about each verse as it comes along and then linking the verses together to see what the whole lot really mean, you will see Mary's humility simply shining out from the text. You will come to understand an important thing about humility — that it is not a matter of letting people walk over your face but a matter of knowing the truth about yourself. Humility is not just sitting limp, belittling yourself. It is not saying 'I'm no good, and shall never be able to do anything worthwhile for either God or man.' It is saying, 'I may be no good or I may be quite good or I may be very good. If I am no good, God can still use me and give me the grace to be some good; and if there is some good in me it is God who has put it there.' The good which Mary could see in herself was nothing to be proud of, and it is exactly the same with us. If we use it right we can use that good to make us humble.

Humility, then, is the virtue of seeing ourselves as no better and no worse than we really are. It is not being contemptuous of ourselves — which might be sheer humbug — but being honest about ourselves. If you can swim a mile you are not being humble if you tell people you can just manage to keep afloat. If you are praised for getting ninety marks out of a hundred in an exam, you are not being humble if you say, 'No, no, I scraped through with thirty-five.' To be humble you do not have to lie; all you have to do is to be truthful. You do not have 'to boast of the good things God has given you — boasting is always the reverse of humility — but there is nothing meritorious about denying them. The humble person is the *real* person, never mistaking the imaginary self for the true self.

One of the drawbacks about day-dreaming is that it produces an imaginary self (the hero of a thousand adventures, the saint who is acknowledged by all, the patient soul who is always smiling sweetly when even the nastiest jobs have to be done), and the self which it produces is always on top. In everyday life, that is in *real* life, we spend very little time on top. Perhaps this is because we should so soon get vain if we did, and God knows it is better for us to grind along in low gear. God knows that we would not choose to be humble if we realized all the humilities we would be letting ourselves in for, so He keeps us humbled by the sight of our failings and lets us make a virtue of it.

'Thy humiliation,' says the prophet Michaeas, 'shall be in the midst of thee.' What the prophet means is that we do not learn humility out of books, or from doing menial and degrading things; we learn humility from the inside. We learn it chiefly by allowing the humility of Christ and His mother to develop in our souls. We learn it by coming close to Jesus and Mary in prayer. 'Learn of me because I am meek and humble of heart,' said our Lord. Mary might well have said the same. There is no boasting here: it is the straight-forward appeal to Truth.

The same idea of truth and humility going together can be seen when we give to Mary the title 'Mother of God.' The title is theologically accurate: it states a truth. We know at once that it would be both untrue and unhumble if our Lady were to say 'Oh no, you really must not call me that. I am no more than an ordinary mother, and my baby is no more than an ordinary baby.' Why do we instinctively understand that our Lady could never have said such a thing? Surely it is because instinctively we know that humility is truth, and that Mary was perfect in both those virtues.

Have you ever thought what it must be like to be the mother of God? Although you can never get any real idea of it, you can at least understand how it must add to whatever Mary must have felt as a mother. It added to her joys and it added to her sorrows. Think of the happiness which must have been hers when she saw that her divine Son was being listened to in His preaching, that the love which He inspired among His disciples was divine love, that His tenderness for sinners was divine mercy, that His consideration for herself was something infinitely greater than the natural feeling of a son for His mother.

But think also of the other side of the picture. Imagine what it must have been like to know that in persecuting her son the Jews were blaspheming God, that in doubting His word they were rejecting divine revelation, that in witnessing against Him they were destroying a tradition of centuries and throwing

47

themselves into the darkness of unbelief. We are told that the grief of a mother is the saddest of all griefs, and since the bond between mother and son is the closest of all bonds we can easily accept it as so. But when the Son happens to be God and when the mother happens to be Mary, we know that a new possibility of grief has appeared. We cannot guess what such grief must be like, but we know very well that it stretches beyond all ordinary human experience.

CHAPTER 6

Pray For Us Sinners

THERE IS A VERSE IN the prophecy of Jeremias which has been applied by the Church to our Lady, and it exactly expresses this petition in the *Hail Mary*. The words are: 'Remember, Lord, that I have stood in thy sight to speak good for them, and to turn away thine indignation from them.' So when we ask Mary to plead for us in our sinfulness, we can be absolutely sure that she is standing before the throne of God and begging His mercy. Her prayers are turning away the punishment which we deserve. It is not so much that she is directing the traffic down a side street, but rather that she is meeting the force of it herself. As Mother of Sorrows, she takes upon herself the pains which were really meant for us — and offers them up together with her Son who bore our iniquity and shouldered our guilt.

So long as we admit we are sinners we have a sure claim upon Mary's intercession. The trouble is that we can admit in a general way that we are sinners, but when it comes down to particular sins we can make so many excuses for having committed them that we do not count ourselves having sinned at all. It is no good saying, 'I am a sinner,' which is what everyone is bound anyway to admit if he is not a perfect fool, unless we go on to say, 'and these failures of mine in resisting this and that temptation positively prove it.' The first part of penitence is owning up to guilt. Until we admit that there is something to be sorry for, we cannot begin to be sorry. And until we are sorry it is no good asking for pardon.

One of the greatest evils of the age in which we are now living is the way in which people can become so smug about sin. 'The greatest sin of our generation,' said Pope Pius XII, 'is that it has lost the sense of sin.' Though we do not have to be thinking all day about sin, and telling ourselves how awful we are, we must be on the alert about sin. We must know that we are never far from the occasions of sin, that the devil is always trying to trap us into it, and that the grace to avoid sin is only going to work if we choose to make use of it.

Grace does not act like a magic spell, keeping sin at

bay while we sit about within an enchanted circle and make no effort to resist evil. Nor does it strengthen us if we fool ourselves into saying, 'Everyone seems to commit sins — worse ones than mine — so I am probably safe enough.' A sin is not made less of a sin just because it is committed by everybody. If the whole world went wrong, it would still be your duty to go right. So do not ever imagine that because a bad act is done often enough it is not worth noticing. The devil's main object in this world is twofold: first, to persuade people that sin either does not exist or does not matter; second, to persuade people that there is no such thing as grace, and that therefore it is no good praying for it. The *Hail Mary* contradicts both these ideas, and if we pray it properly, really meaning the words we say, the devil can never have it all his own way with us; Mary will see to that.

After the *Our Father*, the prayer which is most used by the faithful must surely be the *Hail Mary*: the same ideas about sin and temptation can be seen in both. We can well imagine what efforts the devil is making to prevent us from saying these prayers. They are the trip-wires on which he stumbles as he goes about the world trying to draw souls away from God. So long as we pray 'lead us not into temptation . . . deliver us from evil . . . pray for us sinners' we are defeating the devil's plans. The moment we begin to think 'temptation can take the lead for once . . . evil is everywhere so it is no good trying to resist it . . . why bother to ask for

Mary's prayers when there are far worse sinners than
me to pray for?' *then* the devil knows he can take over.

✠

Another thing which the *Hail Mary* has in common
with the *Our Father* is that it is worded in the plu-
ral: we are all praying for each other and not for ourselves alone. The true Christian is not a hoarder of
graces; he is a sharer. The true Christian knows that
when he includes others in his intentions he is not
weakening the force of his own private request but
actually strengthening it. We would make a mistake
if we thought that there was just enough grace to go
round and that unless we grabbed our share quickly
we might have to go without. We would make just
as great a mistake if we thought that by praying for
a great number of souls we were likely to have the
effects of our prayer spread thin. The way to think of
it is as sunshine coming out of the clouds. If there are
a thousand people or only two, the light and warmth
are there for as many as may want to take advantage
of what is going on. One person's enjoyment of the
sunshine does not lessen the light and warmth for
someone else.

So When we pray to Mary, asking her to intercede
for all who have sinned, we are adding the virtue of
charity to the virtue of religion. While every prayer is
an act of charity as far as the love of God is concerned,
the prayers which have our neighbours' needs included

in them are of a double charity. So we can only suppose that this second kind of charity, which asks for graces to be shared by others, is doubly pleasing to God. 'Pray for us sinners' — and we can mention by name as many of our fellow sinners as we like. 'Pray for us sinners' — and we can sweep in the whole unnumbered family of mankind. 'Pray for us sinners' — and we have the comforting knowledge that we ourselves are finding a place in the countless *Hail Marys* of other people which are going up to heaven from all over the world.

Nowhere do you get a better idea of all that we have been considering in this chapter than at Lourdes. Here at her shrine, where for a century the *Hail Mary* has been the theme-tune of the faithful's devotion, you can see how all that we are told about our Lady fits in. It is like seeing the prophecies come true, like watching the theory come to life, like finding a hundred different shafts of light caught in a single beam — and brought to bear upon a point of light which is light itself, Mary's Son.

Not only do you see at Lourdes the wonder of a universal Church at its prayer to the Mother of God, but you see how the Mother of God hands on that prayer to her divine Son. 'Through Mary to Christ' is the key to the story of Lourdes, and it is the key to the whole of the Church's teaching about Mary. Those who think that too much homage is paid to Mary in the Catholic Church should visit the place where more homage is given to her than anywhere else, and they will see that she keeps none of it for herself. It all goes straight on from our Lady to our Lord. The highlight of the Lourdes timetable is not the procession of torches but the procession of the Blessed Sacrament. Even greater than the marvel of miracles is the marvel of conversions, confessions, communions. Far from hoarding the devotion of the faithful, Mary brings it to focus upon the Mass. If the grotto and the baths are a rallying point for pilgrims, the tabernacle is their goal. If the *Ave, Ave, Ave Maria* is the hymn most often repeated during the day, it is followed, when sung last thing at night, by the Creed. If visits of devotion are paid to various places inside and outside the town, it is the Stations of the Cross on the side of the hill that are felt to be more important and that are better remembered afterwards. Mary leads her pilgrims to the mysteries of Christ's life, to the sacraments of Christ's Church, to the practice of Christ's teaching.

So if you remember nothing else from this book than the fact that Mary stands between your soul and God, bringing Him to you and you to Him, you will not have wasted your time in reading it. The praise which you give to her is not praise taken off your debt of praise to God; the grace which she brings to you is not a lesser kind of grace than what you might be getting from God. And when people ask you, 'Why not deal with God directly?' the answer you can give is: 'For the same reason that God, in bringing redemption to man, did not deal with us directly. If He chose

Mary to be the channel of His grace to me, I cannot
be wrong in choosing her to be a channel of my prayer
to Him. If He gave to Mary greater privileges than
to any other woman since the world began,
I cannot be wrong in following
suit—giving to her a homage
beyond that which I
would give to any
other saint.'

CHAPTER 7

Now

E WHO LIVE IN an age which wants things done at once (we jump at instant heating, instant laundry, instant cooking) can see what was in the minds of our ancestors when they drew up the last part of the *Hail Mary*. It is comforting to think that they were as impatient as we are to catch our Lady's attention and beg her instant prayer.

It is as though we were saying to her; 'I know you have been praying for us all for centuries, and that until the end of the world your prayer will go on mounting up for sinful man. But this, true as I know it to be, seems a far off idea. As for me, I am concerned with the present moment. So I ask that you should pinpoint

your prayer, and focus it upon the here and now. I ask
that you should pray for us today.'

Again you see an echo of the *Our Father*, where we
ask that we be given '*this* day our daily bread.' It is
instinctive in all of us to want a quick return of our
effort, and it is just as instinctive to feel that time may
run out before we get the graces which we need. We
shall be asking again tomorrow, and the day after, but
in the meantime there is something urgent going on
right in front of us. So Mary, 'pray for us now.'

And even if what is going on in front of us does
not seem to be so very urgent — in fact if it is just an
ordinary sort of day — there is still every reason why
the help of Mary's prayer should be asked for now. It is
not only in the great affairs of life that we turn to Mary
for support, intercession, prompting. Obviously when
we have serious decisions to make, violent temptations
to fight, deep sorrows to meet, we should look to our
blessed mother for grace and say our *Hail Marys* with
special meaning. But that 'now' applies to ordinary
everyday things as well.

If we really treated our Lady as our mother, would
we not be calling upon her pretty well all day long? The
child wants to be picked up *now* by its mother, wants
to be lifted off its high chair *now* by its mother, wants
to be taken for a drive *now*, wants to be tucked in *now*:
the mother is doing something for the child morning,
noon, and night. What she is doing may not be terribly
important in itself, but the point is that the child needs

her and that she loves doing things for the child. So these ordinary things which she does *become* important. Every 'now' is important in one way or another, so we pray that Mary may be with us to handle it.

With a little effort we can get into the way of covering all the happenings of life with this one-word prayer from the *Hail Mary*. While we are trying to make up our minds, for instance, about how to spend the afternoon, or about what to read, about whom to invite to a party: Mary can guide us here. When we have a headache, when it is raining and we want to go out, when we have work to do which interferes with something else, when we have a letter to write and we do not know what to say; Mary can help with each of these.

It is always now, one instant after another, and the mistake we make is to waste these nows by letting them slip along without noticing them spiritually. Think how pleasing to God a whole string of passing nows could be if we gave even a few of them just that slight spiritual push which would keep them directed towards Him. It would be no good trying to do this all the time — because we would go crazy if we said 'now, now, now' for long — but at least every now and then during the day we could remind ourselves that what is going on, however unexciting the thing is, has the mark of God's will upon it. This being so, we need Mary's prayers *now* — so that we may bring this moment of God's will to perfection.

✠

There is also another kind of 'now' on which we need our Lady's blessing — the bigger and wider 'now' of the times in which we live. To pray for the world as it is now, when everything seems more mixed up than ever before, is a most worthwhile prayer. It has the added merit of being proof against selfishness. You and I have very little to gain personally from the granting of such a prayer — except in the sense that we gain grace from every prayer we say — so to pray for the state of the world as it is at present must be especially pleasing to God for the largeness of its charity.

In such an intention we include all the needs which are crying out from so many parts of the globe. We are praying for those who have not got enough to eat, for those who are unable to practise their religion, for those who are at war, for the poor, the tempted, and the sick. We are praying that Mary may today intercede for her vast family of children in such a way that heresy, indifference, worldliness, greed — all the evils of our time — may give way to a desire for better things in the world. We are praying that the mood of modern man may change. Mary, pray for us sinners now — that we may come to see the truth about God's creation. Pray for us that we may love and not hate, that we may be at peace and not at war. Pray for us today.

✠

We read in history how on two occasions (probably

on a lot more than two occasions but at least on these two very important ones) European Christianity was rescued from invasion by the intercession of Mary. The first time was in 1571 when the sea battle of Lepanto saved the Western Church from being overrun by unbelieving Turks. The second time was a century later when the land battle of Vienna in 1683 again won the day for the followers of Christ. One sea battle; one land battle. Perhaps the next battle which Mary will help Christianity to win will take place in the air. Anyway we cannot go wrong in asking Mary to pray for the future of mankind now, before things get any worse.

But we do not ask her to save us only from our enemies, from what threatens us when we look across to the other side of the Iron Curtain. We ask her to save us from the evil in our midst, from evils which threaten just as much as communism does but in a different way. We ask to be delivered from the false ideas which have got into the heads of so many Christian people, and which are ruining Christian souls. We ask that Mary may implant the ideals and standards of the Gospel, that she may turn away the morals which are not of Christ, that she may lead men and women, boys and girls, back to a purer and stricter way of life.

Remember how in her appearances at Fatima, our Lady accused us Catholics of failing in the matter of purity. Sins against this virtue were increasing, she said, and reparation would have to be made. Unless we uphold the principles of holy purity, the world will so wear down the idea of modesty that nothing will be left. It is for us Catholics to be firm about this virtue, and to show by the strictness of our behavior that we are taking our lead from Jesus and Mary. Holy Mary, mother of God, pray for us sinners now — when morals are so slack and there is a false liberty in the world — or we shall be overrun by a worse evil than communism. We shall be overrun by the evil of worldliness. Worldliness is all the more dangerous as an evil because it is mostly inside us. The evils which are outside us we can fight against more easily; it is the ones that spring up within our own hearts that most need conquering.

⚜

CHAPTER 8

And at the Hour of Our Death

*T*HERE ARE ONLY
two moments in our lives which
are absolutely certain, and at both
of them we need our Lady's help.
One of these moments is now, and the
other is the moment of our death. All other moments
escape us; we cannot pin them down. The past is finished,
and out of our control. The future has not come yet,
and we do not know what it is going to bring. So all we
have to work upon is the present, and all we can be sure
of is that one day we shall die. The chapter before this
one had a lot to say about the present, so from now
onwards the rest of the book is going to be about death.

The way most people think about death is
crazy. They picture themselves either lying in bed

surrounded by weeping relatives, or lying in the middle of a road surrounded by police, ambulances, and shocked passers-by. Sometimes they think of themselves as drowning in a lake, sometimes as burning in a fire. But mostly it is a choice between the deathbed and the car (or plane) crash. How real this picture is to the people who imagine it will depend upon their mental powers of building up a scene. But this is the one thing which the thought of death should not depend upon.

The thought of death should depend upon trust in God's Providence. We should get used to the *idea* of death, but it is not the least good trying to get used to the *picture* of death. We have not the faintest notion of how death will come, or where we shall be, or who will be there. So the most sensible thing to do about it is to pray that we may be ready for it when the time arrives. For this reason the last clause in the *Hail Mary* is a very sensible and practical prayer indeed.

The more practical our thinking is on this subject the better; getting worked up about it does no good at all. Death is not something we can practise beforehand. We are not given a script and told to learn our lines. The part we play is a 'blind' part. But though we cannot, as an actor might rehearse the act in a play, study the role of ourselves dying *we can go into training for it*. We can prepare for a good death by leading a good life. We can make sure of doing this all-important thing well by facing the certainty of it, by leading up to it with a faithful observance of our duties as Catholics, by not running away from it, and by praying that the grace of God may shelter us from last minute blunders.

People who are so scared of death that they never dare give a thought to it will find themselves faced at the end with something puzzling and alarming. There would be hardly any puzzle or alarm if they 'had prepared themselves by a life-long expectation of it. You do not have to say, I had better think about death for a bit,' because that might become habit-forming and unhealthy, but there is no need to push away the thought of it when it comes into your head. The more you can think of death as bringing about a fuller and more perfect form of life, the less you will want to stifle the certain knowledge that it is coming nearer every day. The saints looked forward quite naturally to death, and make no fuss either about thinking of it regularly or not thinking about it enough. It was a living reality in the background of their minds, and that is the way it ought to be with us.

So you see it is a mistake to dwell mournfully upon the chances of making a bad death. You should dwell confidently upon the chances of making a good one. The thing to get right is trust. Trust in God's mercy. Though it would be presumption to stretch trust so far as to feel safe about death however sinful a life you might decide to lead, it would certainly not be presumption to count on God's mercy for the forgiveness of sins which you are sorry for when you come to die. If you get the virtue of hope right, you do not have to stray over the border into presumption.

Nor do you have to worry, with hope growing inside you every day, about despair. If the thought of death gives you even a twinge of despair, it is a thought which has to be corrected with a careful and constant application of hope. Souls who dwell on the idea of God's mercy do not panic at the prospect of death. They can say this last sentence of the Hail Mary quite calmly and happily. *Pray for us at the hour of our death. Amen.* They have nothing to fear: Mary will be there.

It is the custom among certain tribes in Africa to prepare for death by dressing up. While the dying are still fully conscious they are made aware, by the attentions paid to their appearance, of what they are in for. Strings of beads are placed round their necks, and if the dying person is a man he is given his spear and shield to hold; women when dying are crowned with their bridal crown of charms and medals, and in their hands are placed little images of their gods. The beads, the medals, the crown: suitable adornments with which to come before the throne of God. The spear and shield: suitable protection against the evil spirits which lie in wait at the soul's departure.

What these things mean to tribesmen in Africa, the rosary should mean to us. When the time comes for us to die we should turn instinctively to the beads of the rosary (which is also called the *corona* or crown). The rosary is our spear and shield in whatever attack the devil may mount against us before the end. The crucifix, the figure of our God upon the cross, will be in our hands. Think how real the *Hail Mary* will be on that day: 'Pray for us now' we shall say, 'which is the day of our death. Amen.' When the 'now' and the 'death' come together, this prayer to our Lady will truly come into its own. We have nothing to fear: Mary is never more a mother of mankind than when caring for the sinful and the dying. And if when the hour comes we are so tired and weak as to be unable to do much in the way of prayer, we can put a slightly different meaning upon the word 'for.' 'Pray for us sinners — instead of us sinners as well as on behalf of us sinners . . . because we sinners have neither the energy nor the wisdom nor the generosity to pray well enough for ourselves.'

Also available from
AROUCA PRESS

Meditations for Each Day
Antonio Cardinal Bacci (pbk *&* hb)

Fraternal Charity
Fr. Benoît Valuy, S.J.

The Epistle of Christ:
Short Sermons for the Sundays of the Year
on Texts from the Epistles
Fr. Michael Andrew Chapman